MW01171887

TABLE OF CONTENTS

FOREWORD

Pastor Taurus Johnson does an impeccable job of capturing the reality of the pain associated with grief and turning it inside out. He offers a biblical perspective that doesn't just ease the pain, it replaces it with an inner joy and excitement about the wonderful things in store for those that belong to God.

"Precious in the sight of the LORD is the death of his saints" (Psalm 116:15). This book embraces this truth in a way that makes it easily comprehensive for the reader. Pastor Johnson uses very practical illustrations to convey his message. His candor and vulnerability give us a front row seat, experiencing how a man's grief and sadness was turned to joy and hope right before our very eyes.

May your unbearable pain be replaced with gratitude and gratefulness as God reveals His undying love for you like never before.

"For which cause we faint not; but though our outward man perish, yet the inward man is renewed day by day.

For our light affliction, which is but for a moment, worketh for us a far more exceeding and eternal weight of glory;"

2 Corinthians 4:16-17

Foreward by:

Dr. Hosea Collins

Senior Pastor

Calvary Baptist Church, Hawthorne, CA

PREFACE

"Death comes often but it's always a stranger." These words I have heard said by my father a number of times whenever someone we knew would pass away. It wasn't until I was a little older that I really could understand the depth of this expression. Perhaps you are like I was as a young child hearing it wondering what in the world does that mean. It simply means that for the person who has just lost a loved one there is no amount of preparation nor is there ever enough time spent with the loved one that death doesn't hit you with a raw crash of emotions. Intense waves of anger, hurt, vulnerability, sadness, depression, grief, confusion, emptiness feelings of despair, and loneliness can all come crashing into the life of the bereaved all at once.

The unfortunate truth is, not to sound morbid, but the death of someone close to us is something we all have or will have to deal with and navigate our way through at some point and time. The only way to not be affected by someone's loss is to never love.

In my 52 years of life I've lost my father, a spiritual father (Pastor) with whom I was very close, aunts, uncles, friends, teammates, and classmates. Now as I am writing this book, I am approaching three years since my mother went home to be with the Lord. Her homegoing literally rocked me to my core. It was in the midst of this time of mourning that God revealed to me that many others are dealing with this same type of grief. Don't just tell them I got you out, as our math teacher would sometimes instruct us when giving us a test, show your work!

After some time through much prayer, meditation, and instruction from my pastor (whom I consider one of God's greatest funeral orators) I was reawakened to what The Word says to do about navigating through periods of intense grief and anguish. It is of the utmost importance to take control of what we allow our minds to dwell on. When Jesus said Let not your heart be troubled, (John 14:1) He wasn't giving a suggestion. He didn't say, oh I've got an idea that might help you out a little. He was giving instructions. Then He followed that statement up by telling them what to allow their hearts to focus on. Imagine this dialog as it went on in real time at that moment. In essence He tells them this, "If you trust me like you've been trusting in God; and you focus on the fact, that my Father's house is not just a mansion, my Father's house has many mansions! He might have seen a bit of confusion or doubt on their faces with that statement so He hurries and follows it up by saying in so many words, hey you know me I wouldn't even tell you that if it wasn't true. So, since my Father's house has many mansions I am going to make sure that everything is prepared for you when it's your time to come.

The main point I'm trying to make is that Jesus, who is God our creator in human flesh (remember no one knows how a created thing was intended to function like its creator) demonstrates a principle. He first tells them not to let their hearts be troubled. So, He paints them a picture with his words (because words produce pictures) of what to focus on.

It was out of this revelation that I began to understand that the way to combat a troubled heart is to produce new pictures for the heart to focus on. The following pages will simply share with you, some pictures that God has shared with me that shift our perspectives of the loss of our loved ones. With shifting perspectives our minds change, our hearts heal and what was weakness can become our strength. It is my prayer that you don't read this book as just another book but that you allow God to change the picture you've been seeing as it relates to the death of the ones you love.

By faith and love I pronounce the healing of your heart, and the creation of new perspectives which move you to wholeness very area In the name of Jesus! Amen!

Chapter 1
There is Hope

To really get true deliverance from overwhelming grief when it comes to the death of a loved one there are certain spiritual principles that we must first understand.

Psalms 119:130 reads this way:

130 The entrance of thy words giveth light; it giveth understanding unto the simple.

So, we can see that two major characteristics of The Word of God are 1. It gives light, and 2. It gives understanding. For this reason, we should always allow the wisdom of God's Word to give us our perspective on all issues of life. Since this is true that also means that if we don't get God's perspective and view things through the lens of His Word, we can be operating in what seems like wisdom and common sense, but we will actually be operating in darkness or ignorance. Ignorance is not a bad word, nor is it a word meant to ridicule or degrade anyone. Ignorance simply means to operate without knowledge!

Keeping this in mind we must see things through God's perspective in order for our lives to manifest His best in every area of our lives. When we can't change what we are seeing, if it is unpleasant or even painful then it's to our benefit to change how we look at it. The Bible is simply a book of God's perspective (Gods viewpoint) on every area of life. God doesn't want us to be so bound down with the sorrow and grief from the loss of a loved one that we can't function or that it takes away from the overall joy and peace of our lives even after a normal season of mourning.

One key to being able to do this is to keep the proper (Gods) perspective on what happens when our loved ones leave this life in death. 1 Thessalonians 4:13 reads:

But I would not have you to be ignorant brethren concerning them which are asleep, that ye sorrow not, even as those who have no hope. (1 Thes 4:13 KJV)

Therefore, the key to not being overwhelmed with sorrow is found in the knowledge of what Paul (the author) is about to tell us.

To farther explain the Bible talks about 3 forms of death. There is 1. Physical death, 2. Spiritual death and 3. Eternal death.

The first is the one we are most familiar with and the purpose of this book. Physical death is simply when the spirit and the soul exit the body. Gen. 2:7 says that God breathed into man's nostrils the breath of life (breath of life = the spirit, with a functioning operating system called the soul) and he became a living soul.

The second form of death is the spiritual death. It is separation from God. Since He (God) is the source and sustainer of all life; then separation from the life source means death. Note that God had promised death to Adam and Eve if they ever ate of the tree in the midst of the garden, yet Adam didn't die physically until he was over 900 years old. The death that Adam died as a result of his disobedience was spiritual separation from his life sustainer.

The third type of death talked about in the Bible is eternal death which is eternal damnation and banishment into the lake of fire forever.

We will explain all of these in much greater detail in Volume 2 of this book. However, what Paul was saying in 1 Thessalonians 4:13 and the following verses. was essentially this. If we understand that true death is not when our loved ones have departed this life in what we normally call death. True death is being separated from The Sustainer of life itself and no matter what realm of existence you are in physical or spiritual when you are connected to God you are alive eternally. For that reason the Bible says to be absent from the body (in the physical existence) is to be present with God (in spiritual existence). If you are in a room with someone and they leave to go into another room, it doesn't mean they are gone from the house. You won't start to cry, be depressed or be lonely knowing that they are just in the other room where you can't see them. Likewise our loved ones are still alive they just exist in a realm that we can't see with our physical eyes.

(Note *Jeremiah 1:5 before I formed thee...*) –This confirms that the spirit is more eternal than the physical body. Therefore according to God's promises (in His Word) if your loved one had a relationship with God through Jesus Christ they are alive. Here is a great irony, many times we see funerals crowded with people mourning the loss of a loved one. The sad thing is sometimes the one in the casket is more alive than those mourning them, because they had received Jesus Christ and have a relationship with God.

Our great Hope that we can anchor to when it comes to the loss of a loved one is that the Hope of eternal life through Jesus Christ. What an amazing blessing knowing that there is no death when we are connected to our Creator, Source and Sustainer.

If you have not made that amazing connection and come to know Jesus Christ as your Lord and Savior. You may do so by praying this prayer with me.

Heavenly Father I believe Jesus Christ is your only begotten son. I believe He came and died for my sins. Jesus, I receive you now as my Lord and

Savior. Please come into my heart and help me live my life pleasing you and fulfilling your purpose for me. In the name of Jesus, Amen.

CHAPTER 2
THE AIRPORT

One of the most hurtful things about the death of one we love is the fact that we have a hard time wrapping our minds around what our lives might be like without them in it. What will our new normal be like? What will it feel like?

For several years I had been my mother's caretaker. Even on trips to the store or running errands to take care of business I always made it a point not to stay long so I could hurry back to be here if she needed me.

This went on for years. It became normal. I would get something to eat and rarely sit down to eat in a restaurant just getting food to go because I wanted to get back in case she needed my help.

So, when she passed away, I remember the first few times that I went somewhere and sat down to eat. I couldn't help but feel guilty because this was now a new normal, I was having to adjust to.

It's been three years since she went home to be with the Lord, and I still sometimes remind myself when I buy food not to buy an extra plate to take home for her. The first few times this happened it was definitely a trigger and the hurt and grief followed. Now if it happens, I smile and think or mention to my wife this is good food, mama would have loved this.

Yes, we have difficulty imagining them not in our lives currently, but what's better to know is that they are in our future!

I was in the airport on the way to the funeral services of a beloved family member. As I walked through the terminal on the way to my gate my eyes became fixed on the screen of arriving and departing flights. God began to speak to me. What do you notice He asked me. These flights are arriving soon and those on the other screens are departing soon. As I stood fixated on the screens knowing God was trying to show me more (because God's questions are never because He doesn't know they are to teach us a lesson) Stopping longer to ponder what He was trying to reveal to me. He said the flights departing here have a specific destination, and at the

Airport wherever they are going are screens similar to these except the flights which say departing here, are on the arriving screens there. The flights on the arriving screens here were on a departing screen where they left from. He went on to reveal, just like you are departing to another city now, in a few days you will be back on a flight coming into this same airport, but your plane then will be on the arriving screen. The Holy Spirit took me immediately to the scripture:

8 We are confident, yes, (A)well pleased rather to be absent from the body and to be present with the Lord. 2 Cor. 5:8 KJV

With this scripture God was literally giving us His departure and arrival screen! When our loved ones depart from this life their arrival is in the presence of the Lord! (Glory to God!)

God went on to show me that just like you are coming back here in a few days although you purchased a ticket and will travel across the country on a round trip. My children's tickets purchased when they receive Jesus as their Lord and Savior is a round-trip ticket. They will be back and I'm coming with them!

Even on this return trip they aren't coming back to stay at this time, but we will be together again. Their spirits and souls which have been with the Lord are coming back with him to get together with all those who haven't gone to be with the Lord yet! And the Bible says that at that moment the bodies which had been deposited in the Earth, some for hundreds even thousands of years are going to reassemble and be changed within fractions of a second to a brand-new glorified body (without pains, problems or defects) ready and suited for the Heavenly Kingdom. At the same time those who are alive will be changed (into their brand-new glorified body) and caught up with them in the air! The greatest reunion you could ever imagine! Right there in the air with our loved ones and Jesus. What a glorious reunion! If I were you, I would make plans to attend!

Dear Heavenly Father, please help me to live reminded of the great hope that I will be reunited with my loved ones and you when you return. Please help me to be ready for that great time. In the name of Jesus, Amen.

Chapter 3
Coming Back Again

I remember so vividly when I was about 4 years old growing up in the country down a little long dirt road. Our little house was between two hills to our east and west. Traffic from cars was very seldom and far between. It was not uncommon to go throughout an entire day and only see two or three cars pass by our house and they would usually be neighbors going to or coming back in from work.

One day outside riding my little bike 12-inch wheels training wheels and all I had begged my mom to come out and ride with me. My mom at one time loved to exercise daily and having not exercised for quite some time she was looking forward to getting back into exercising again. She decided to bring her bike out into the road in front of the house. We lined up, side by side. Me and my mama are ready to ride. As we started, I remember pushing on my little pedals hard around and around mom started pedaling soon she was moving off ahead of me quite a good distance I tried and tried but couldn't keep up. Soon my mom was much farther down the road. The next thing I knew she was riding over the hill east of our house. I remember feeling mad at first that I couldn't keep up. Then I began to feel alone although I was still right out in front of my house at 4 years old, the world can be a big place! I started to cry as mom rode out of sight over the hill. I felt all alone and frightened as I stood there crying for what seemed like forever. In actuality it was only a few minutes. Soon I saw her head over the crest of the hill through the tears in my eyes. With each push of the pedal, I saw more and more of her until she was over the hill and coming down toward me closer and closer. Mom rode up beside me and in that sweet compassionate voice that only a mom could speak, she said "what's the matter why are you crying? Didn't I tell you I was coming back?" I don't think I ever really answered her. But I remember throughout the years wondering why I cried. Knowing that my mom would never leave or abandon me.

Sometimes I imagine that's the question Jesus wants to ask many of us perhaps its why he told us that it's ok to sorrow but don't sorrow like you don't have hope. I can imagine him saying, didn't I promise you that I am coming back, and your loved ones will be with me when I return? I know you'll miss them. I know you sometimes feel lonely and vulnerable, but instead of focusing on those feelings why not focus on the amazing time you and your loved ones will have with me when we return.

Thinking like this changes the way you see your season of grief. As Jesus already told us we can sorrow because we will miss our loved one. We can cry because we will miss our loved ones, but those tears and sorrow have a different foundation to them. Those tears and emotions don't consume us. We are not in total despair because His promise is our foundation and strength. A cry from a place of strength and a cry from a place of great despair, loneliness and desolation are totally different. When we cry, we don't cry as if we have no hope, we cry in hope that our loved ones are gone away from us for a season, but we are already looking forward to our being together again when Christ returns. Everything about our bereavement changes when our mindsets change.

Have you ever noticed how some people can go through bereavement, and it leads them into a total depression and a seemingly downward spiral. Then some others can lose a loved one and go through a season of bereavement and come out inspired and more focused on living life. Maybe they even chose to work with a cause or charity in honor of their dearly departed loved one. This can only happen when we determine where we will let our minds rest as it relates to our loved ones passing. No, it does not mean we don't love and will miss them tremendously, and it definitely does not mean we won't hurt. There is no denial of the grief and morning we go through. However, the pain and emptiness begins to heal when we Live with the hope of knowing that our loved one is coming back again.

Dear Heavenly Father please help me not to sorrow as if I don't have hope. Help me to always keep your Word in mind that promises that my loved ones are coming back with you. Please help me that I may be ready when you return. In the name of Jesus, Amen.

CHAPTER 4
FRUIT OVER FEELINGS

A couple of years ago I prepared for the Mother's Day message to show God our appreciation for the mothers He has placed in our lives. Both those who are our biological mothers and those who have loved us with a mothering love. My desire was to honor mothers and to make others take an introspective look at their relationship with their mothers and appreciate them even more. I couldn't help but start to have an emotional moment as I began to think of all of the great characteristics of mothers and reflect on my own mother and her unending selfless love! I couldn't help but remember her strength and support, also her corrections and lessons. Before I knew it, I was in a deep place of hurt and missing my mother. I had stopped studying and was just sitting staring at the wall for what seemed like hours. I remember going to lay down thinking that I'd drift off to sleep and when I wake up my mood might be lighter or at least I'd be better able to finish preparing the message. (that's how God moves with me at times) If something is bothering me, I literally pray about it and go to sleep, trusting Him to fix it and speak to me and by the time I awake God has either lifted my burden or given me a revelation often ministering to me in my sleep. This time when I awakened, I was fine and began again preparing for Sunday's message. As I was doing so God began to speak to me and show me a revelation that I pray blesses you as much as it did me.

God reminded me that He loves us so much that He gives us choices. Then He asked me Is it more important for you to bear fruit, or to stay in a state of hurt, anger, and longing for your mother? I was stunned by the question, but I knew God had more there to say. Whenever God asks you a question, it's never for His benefit, it is for ours and our understanding. God went on to ask me: what farmer do you know that plants seed and never watches their field anxiously expecting harvest. He immediately showed me my mother, father, grandmother, pastor, aunts and uncles sowing lesson after lesson into my life, teaching me principles and values. Teaching me respect, humility, honesty, love and most of all teaching me about Him. I saw mom as she helped cultivate my relationship with Him. How she prepared me for where I am today by seemingly having me speak on every church program that there was an opportunity to speak at as a child. I remember how frustrated I used to get not understanding that she saw something in me that she believed God would use some day and she was doing her part as my mother to help nurture and develop it. She told me this many times and I heard her, but I didn't understand it like I do today. God showed me that my mom was sowing precious seeds into my life with every lesson, through every coaching session as she would have me go over my part over and over again much to my frustration. Then God said your life and the fruit you produce will be either a wonderful tribute to her and all those who sowed into you, or it will be an area of unfruitfulness and baren because you allowed the hurt, bitterness, and loneliness of missing them to poison the seeds they have sown.

My whole mentality changed. I literally felt my mind leap into action to get busy producing fruit that is worthy of all that has been deposited in me, by my mother, my father, my pastor, my aunts and uncles, teachers, coaches, friends and all those who God has allowed to sow into my life. I determined that my honor of her and them was more important than to indulge in my pity party until I was bogged down in depression, hurt and bitterness.

Perhaps you've had a loved one who has helped nurture things in you that you never imagined you would become but today here you are. What a blessing to be able to share your gift with others knowing that you might not have become that without that loved one, that teacher, that coach, or that mentor. As you do so the essence of their lives lives on in you. It allows their teachings their thoughts, their words and the time they invested to continue to live on past their time here on Earth in the physical world.

We all know people who never got over the loss of a loved one. Some we say literally grieved themselves to an earlier death. Some became bitter, mad with the world. Some fearful and lonely and some literally seemed to give up on life itself after their loved one passed away.

I pray that as you read this, you see how the tactics of the enemy are very crafty. They are subtle. God doesn't mind us grieving in fact He tells us in His Word that there is a time to morn. (Ecc 3:4) Please as you go through your season of morning consider the many treasured seeds you received from your loved one's life and allow your love and memories of them to grow those things in you that they taught you. By doing this, our beloved legacy never dies but lives on through us as our lives continue to produce fruit of the precious seeds they sowed into us!

Heavenly Father, please help me that I might be able to take knowledge of and focus on the precious seeds that you so strategically have allowed to be sown into my life by loved ones and others so that I may produce fruit and fulfill the purpose for which you have created me. In the name of Jesus, Amen

Chapter 5
It's The Life For Me
(The Blow)

As I'm writing this, I think back about this day 21 years ago my whole life changed. I had torn the patellar tendon in my right knee in a freak accident fishing of all things. That happened on a Tuesday, on Saturday night of that week my mother called us my wife answered the phone I could hear the concern in her voice she got off the phone and said baby get dressed we've got to go over to your mom's house she said she can't get your dad to wake up. Long story short, my dad had a massive stroke. It would be on Monday May 5th that I was scheduled for surgery to repair my knee, and he was in the VA hospital across town. When I woke up after my surgery, I found my family standing around my bed. The first question out of my mouth how is dad? My wife grabbed my hand, and she said baby dad didn't make it he passed away.

I remember thinking immediately that I needed to be strong for my mom and help comfort her all the while inside I felt like my whole world had crumbled. Here was the man my Earthly hero whom I had never seen let sickness get him down. Years previously even when he was recovering from heart valve replacement surgery, he never took anything for pain and the doctors were astonished at how quickly he recovered and was back on his feet.

So even with the doctors saying he had a massive stroke I still couldn't see him not overcoming it and bouncing back.

For some of us that becomes the way Satan uses what happens to our loved ones around the time of their death to hurt us the most. It's the big blow, the person was doing just fine but all of a sudden something happens, and they pass away. Or the doctors give a good report that the person is recovering, and things change suddenly. Sometimes the shock comes because you just spoke to the person a day or two ago, or sometimes just hours before. Maybe it's the tragedy of a loved one passing away in the horrible accident, or what about the precious life of a young innocent child who seemingly hasn't begun to live the best of their lives yet and a sudden tragedy occurs.

We must understand that Satan does his best work in the realm of our emotions. Therefore, sometimes suddenly is sometimes another tool he uses against the living. He can no longer hurt the dead, but he will gladly use the circumstances around their death to torment us and keep us burdened and depressed over what has happened.

So, what do I do on this day when I remember the pain of what happened? Instead of choosing to remember the agony of the one day he left I purposely make myself remember the 14,235 days that I had with him. (I was 39 when he passed away 39 x 365 = 14,235) My dad was a fun loving, people loving person. He never met a stranger and if he did, they wouldn't be for long. He loved to talk, sing, and joke. My dad was custodian at the high school I attended growing up. I can remember a number of days hearing him singing as he drove the tractor cutting the grass. You could actually hear him over the tractor. Then it was so embarrassing. Now it's one of those precious memories. My good friend Dr. Ronnie Morris says the things that aggravate and frustrate us about our friends and loved ones the most while they are living are the things that we miss the most once they are gone. No, I can't keep myself from remembering that day; but I get to choose how it dwells on it and him. It's a dishonor to how much I love him and to how he loved to live life to let all of my 14,235 days with him be overshadowed by 1 day in which he was no longer here with me physically.

Jesus indicated that God gives us a choice of what we allow our minds to dwell on when he said:

Let not your heart be troubled: ye believe in God, believe also in me. (John 14:1)

The words "let not" indicate that we have a choice. The beautiful thing about the God we serve is that if we determine to do it, He will help us!

So, I can choose to dwell on him leaving or dwell on his living. I choose living, it's the living for me!

I pray that as you read this and you reflect on your loved one(s) who have passed on, you remember that the amount of time you had them is far too precious to be tainted by one day. May the memories of the days you enjoyed continue to uplift you.

Dear Lord please help me focus on the blessing of my loved one's life and the precious days you gave us together instead of the pain of their death. Your Word says to let not my heart be troubled please help me replace the troubling with precious memories of our time together in Jesus's name Amen.

CHAPTER 6
WHEN THE GRIEF TURNS TO GRUDGES

I t has been said that funerals are one of the things that bring people together and tear them apart most. We've all heard countless stories and maybe seen it play out in our own family, those situations where families are left fractured after the loss of a loved one. Not just fractured by the grief, the pain, the loneliness after the loss of their loved ones, but fractured from the dispute, infighting and bickering that comes afterward. No doubt in some way or form this situation has reared its head in many of our families at one time or another whether close or extended family this contagion spreads far too often and knows no bounds. It doesn't discriminate due to a family's age, race, religion, socio-economic status, or location.

It attacks all career fields and is all too common in the educated as well as uneducated. It rears its head in

Christian and non-Christian families. This virus of negative emotions and consequences knows no boundaries and stops at nothing. The sad irony is that it has often destroyed the very fabric of the family who could actually be greater strength and support to each other if they were to stick together in love and unity.

33 For God is not the author of, confusion but of peace, as in all churches of the saints. (1 Cor 14:33)

So since we see from the scripture that the source of confusion quarrels and disputes is not God then we understand that it can only come from one other source that source is Satan. When we consider this some important questions leap to the forefront to be answered. What is it that the enemy of our souls has discovered about the human psyche especially during the time of mourning that allows him to launch such devastating attacks over the bows of our family bonds and ties that have been keeping us together. Also, one has to wonder how he has constructed a weapon that is so effective on so many fronts. From the families of the wealthy to the poor. From the corner of the Northwest to the deepest corner of the Southeast. From the rolling plains to the Bible Belt. From the educated to the illiterate how is Satan so effective in his strategy against families in the time where they need each other the most.

Keeping in mind that the next volume of this book will go more in depth from a biblical perspective. The Bible teaches us that Satan's attempted coup of Heaven was a result of one core issue, because iniquity was found in him.

And the unfortunate fact is that in all of his searching and studying of humans and their behavior, could he have noticed even from our infancy that when humans are triggered with intense emotions and hurt, they grasp for something to cling to. As infants it may be mother or father, a binky or teddy bear. The older the individual the larger sometimes literally the object. Especially if it is something with which we have an emotional connection. Perhaps this is the reason family members will fight tooth and nail amongst themselves over an item or items that belonged to their loved one. The object holds memories and connection to the deceased one who they loved so dear. The pain creates the intensity needed to cling to that thing with an even stronger grip and to defend it more passionately against anyone who tries to separate it from them. They holding to the object becomes a metaphor of them trying to hold on to their loved one who has just grievously slipped from their grasp. Therefore, the struggle only plays out over the object. The true struggle is the intense pain, heartache, grief, loneliness and despair the bereaved person may be experiencing. So, the battle is playing out as family member versus family member or one side of the family against the other side of the family yet no matter how many people are involved the fight is actually more each individual person against their own pain, grief and anguish. This is why from the outside people who know these people will be shocked and wonder why they don't just let it go, it's not that serious. It's not worth destroying a family relationship. To the person involved it is because they are emotionally holding on to their lost loved one and every time someone tries to remove that object of remembrance and affection it's like their loved one is slipping from their grasp all over again.

Unfortunately, when money or material possessions are added to the scenario the feuds only seem to intensify. The fight becomes fueled but pain and grief but also aided by the lure of what their lives would be like with the security or the pleasures that the material possessions could provide. Thoughts no longer rest on the strength or love or the blessing the family members can be to each other. No one's focus is upon what a great blessing they could be to each other. Justified or not they become self-motivated, and so intertwined in the web of pain, anger, and hurt until they blindly and intensely must have what they desire by any means necessary.

Here, however, is the greatest danger of all in these cases; and I'm sure everyone who reads this book can think of some family that was fractured during a time of grieving who never was able to come back together. When we read 1 Corinthians 13 often called the love chapter in the Bible, we see that God has his own definition of what love is. (The Bible is God's definition) Many times the behaviors of the family when in dispute are directly contrary to what the God kind of love is. Remembering that the scripture says that we know we have passed from death to life because we love the brethren (John 5:24). The real danger in this is what if death finds one of those with their hearts out of position being outside of their love walk.

7Dear friends, let us love one another, for love comes from God. Everyone who loves has been born of God and knows God. 8 Whoever does not love does not know God, because God is love. (1 John 4:7-8 NIV)

The Bible is very clear as to what our hearts position and stance should be. When you weigh any frustration, any dispute, any grudge, any favorite or valued possession, or any amount of money, what is it that is worth one's relationship with God and potentially their eternal security with him? It's not worth it, don't take the bait.

Choose love, choose life!

Dear Heavenly Father, please help me not be so consumed with my own pain and grief that I hurt, burden or hold grudges against others. Please keep your intense love for me at the forefront of my mind so that my heart clings to you and holds on to you over money, material possessions, or ideals. I believe now according to your Word that you have healed every broken area in my life and your love, strength and peace has filled every void in the name of Jesus, Amen.

Chapter 7
Taking The Hurt Out of The Holidays

In the past few months leading up to the holiday season, I heard several people state the fact that the holidays didn't seem the same, or it doesn't seem like the holidays since the loss of a dear loved one. Some even mention that they cannot get into the festivities of the holiday season because their loved one is not here to share with them. Maybe it was some particular event that they were used to sharing together, or a certain family tradition that was carried out each year. Sometimes yet an all too familiar dish that they liked to cook, or a particular spot that they loved to sit in at the table sometimes all these things missing can trigger deep hurt and pain around the holidays as the sounds, scenes and memories seem to all flood our minds of the wonderful joys of having them here with us, and at the same time of the hurtful void of missing them during the holiday season.

Among the many areas and numerous ways that I miss my dear mother the holidays are sometimes the most challenging for one main reason that stands out above all. Anyone who knew my mother knew that one thing she was known for her cooking. So, I grew up in a home where holiday season meant a house filled with the aroma of so many delicious foods cooking and being prepared. Like many mothers one of the ways my mom showed her love for you was to pour her love and special attention into what she cooked for you. So cooking was a very special thing to her, it was her labor of love to be up all-night preparing Thanksgiving, Christmas and even New Years dinners that she could sit with pride and love and watch her family enjoy it.

This brings us to one of the real issues that many times in the process of grieving we misunderstand. Somehow intentionally or unintentionally as we grieve the loss of someone, we love we often associate our thoughts of them with the pain that is present when we think of them. In efforts to relieve ourselves and protect us from this pain we attempt to push and suppress the frequency of those thoughts of them. Remember when we were kids, and we played with the water hose trying to spray each other or maybe even washing the car with water if we had no spray nozzle, we would place our thumbs over the end of the hose causing the water to come out more forcefully and spray farther. I believe that this is what we experience at times especially around the holidays when we try to suppress or subdue and force out memories and thoughts of our loved ones which could be painful. It's what makes the emotions more intense as they do inevitably come out. Let's face it, it's going to be practically impossible to go through the holidays and never remember those who we've spent those times within the past who have meant so much to us.

I believe that God used my wife, and daughters lead me into an area of deliverance from this pain without any of us knowing the great effect it would have. I believe that using the principle practiced here will help you have healing and deal with grief in this area as well.

As I mentioned earlier, some of my earliest and fondest memories of my home around the holidays were the aroma of so much delicious food being prepared in the kitchen by my mom. In fact, my mom told me that before I was tall enough to see the kitchen counter, she would be rolling out dough for one of her staple dishes monkey breads and she'd see little fingers come up onto the edge of the counter trying to steal some of the dough she was rolling out. (yeah, I liked eating dough) Her monkey bread was a favorite in our home it had a distinctive aroma when being made, it had a distinctive aroma when baking in the oven. In the process of missing my mother through the holidays I was unaware of how much we miss the auxiliary things that contributed to those memories. The sights, the sounds, the smells (a particular sweater, the sound of a voice or a particular song, the smell of the food, or a cologne or perfume.) All of these things contribute to the building of memories and just like pieces of a puzzle it takes each of them to make it complete. Also like a puzzle when a piece is missing it cannot go unnoticed.

Since my mother went home to be with the Lord, my wife has made it a point to make her Monkey Bread recipe every Thanksgiving and Christmas and subconsciously something happened. While I was hurting and missing my mom tremendously; not even wanting to get out of the bed, that familiar aroma crept in the room. At first it flooded my mind and heart with even more memories but before I knew it in the midst of tear-filled eyes, a smile came across my face. Before I knew it, I was out of the bed in the kitchen taking in the smell. Now during the holidays, yes, I still miss my mother but every time the house fills with that aroma, every time we sit down at the table and start to eat, and we grab a piece of Monkey Bread, is like mom is with us all over again.

What am I saying? No of course, bread could never begin to replace my mom. Instead of trying to suppress and keep her out of our minds on holidays which were not working anyway, we started embracing something that was important to her that we shared many great memories around. In that way we still honor her memory and in doing so it makes the holidays easier because it's like we have a part of still mom with us.

Put on your loved one's favorite music, cook their favorite dish, go to their favorite event or celebration, maybe even set their place at the table instead of trying to keep their memories out of the holidays let them in embrace them and the steppingstone that they have been in helping you celebrate the holidays. I spoke in the beginning of this book that it was about perspectives simply to help you think of the loss of our loved ones from a different viewpoint. Embrace the holidays from this viewpoint; since we shared so much joy and great memories during the holidays because of my loved one, I'm going to now use their influence to carry on and honor their memory in the holidays by being to others during this holiday season what my loved one was to me. In doing so we create a living legacy and the memories, the love, and the great joy that was the essence of what we received from them never dies.

Dear Heavenly Father, thank you for the influence of our loved ones in our lives. Please help us to take the memories, the love and the lessons and embrace them in a way that heals us and keeps their legacy alive.

CHAPTER 8
DEFEATING DEATH

Through all that was discussed in this book, and through all that we go through in our process of grieving over the transition of our loved ones from their Earthly home to eternal. If not, careful we can get the understanding that death is an ultimate and undefeated foe bringing gloom pain and agony in its wake. An enemy for which no one has any escape.

Can I assure you that nothing could be farther from the truth. Death is a foe, and it is something that every individual must face, but death can be defeated, and Jesus Christ actually gave us the blueprint and the tools to do so. In the Bible

Jesus reveals the blueprint to Martha the sister of His dear friend Lazarus. According to Biblical accounts this is one family that Jesus loved dearly and now they too were experiencing the loss of their brother at the hands of the gloomy foe death. Since the Bible teaches us that

God is not a respecter of persons but that He does respect His Word and His principles we get an opportunity to eavesdrop and benefit from the conversation that Jesus had with one of His most beloved.

The Bible tells us that Lazarus the friend of Jesus had fallen sick, and the family fully expected for Jesus to come and heal him. Yet the Bible says Jesus did something that He often does with us. He had another plan in mind, so He deliberately waited until Lazarus had died to show up. Martha runs to meet Him. I'm sure she was much like we get at times when we feel like Jesus doesn't come through when we expect Him to, hurt, angry, confused, and questioning everything she'd been hearing or believing up to this point. So, she sees Jesus and she says to Him, Master if you had been here our brother would not have died. What Jesus releases to her in His following statements is the arsenal of the Gospel that literally defeats death and the whole plan of the enemy against human life.

25 Jesus said unto her, I am the resurrection, and the life: he that believeth in me, though he were dead, yet shall he live:

26 And whosoever liveth and believeth in me shall never die. Believest thou this?

Jesus literally told Martha, everything you are looking forward to, I AM. Jesus went on to explain to her that true death was the state one is in before they become a believer in Him. Yet once we believe in him, that ends our condition of death. (not to go too deeply into the next volume of this book which is more in depth spiritually) Beloved, death from the biblical perspective (from God's perspective) is separation from Him. Since He gives, sustains and fulfills all life, then separation from Him is essentially death. Some of us have flower beds in our yards, at which certain times each year we must get the weeds and grass out. The moment we pull that grass or those weeds from the soil which gives and sustains its life, it is dead. Though we may not see it turn brown and dry up until days later. The death occurred the moment it was separated from what gave it life. Likewise true death is separation from The Almighty God.

The Bible teaches us clearly that it is Satan's objective to separate us from God through sin.

The blueprint for defeating death is connecting with the source of life who is God. God sent Jesus to pay the price for our sins and to reconnect us to Him. The Jesus said, whosoever believeth in me shall never die. Glory to God, because we are connected to the source of all life!

Most people seem to think that when they get to Heaven, God is going to weigh everything we've done on a big scale and if we've done more good than bad then we will get to enter. May I tell you, friend, that is not the truth. The truth is found in Roman's 10:9 when it says:

Romans 10:9-10

New International Version

⁹ If you declare with your mouth, "Jesus is Lord," and believe in your heart that God raised him from the dead, you will be saved.

Beloved, that is the truth! If your loved one has received Jesus Christ, he has connected them to God! They are now alive forevermore! The Bible tells us that we will see them again one day if we too are connected to The Source. If you have not connected to God and you'd like to see your loved ones again, please pray this prayer with me, and I ask you to pray it aloud because the Bible tells us that our mouths have an important part to pay in our confession.

Heavenly Father, I acknowledge that I have sinned. I acknowledge that I need you to fix the broken areas of my life because I can't do it without you. I believe that Jesus Christ is your Son and that He died for my sins. Jesus please come into my life. I receive you as my Lord and Savior. Please lead me in your purpose and plan so that the rest of my days will be the best of my days. In Jesus's name, Amen.

Congratulations my friend if you've prayed that prayer for the first time you are the newest member of the Body of Christ and you shall see your loved ones again! God bless you!